Reinvention

The Pathway To Job Search Success!

Darrell "Coach D" Andrews, CSP
Certified Speaking Professional
Employment Motivator, Career-Life Coach

Reinvention-The Pathway To Job Search Success

Copyright © 2015 by Passion Publishing And Darrell Andrews

All rights reserved. No part of this book may be reproduced or transmitted in any form or by any means without written permission from the author.

ISBN 978-0-9660103-2-9

Recognition

I would to thank the thousands of organizations that have allowed me and my team of subcontractors to provide training and development, coaching and consulting in the areas of workforce development, school improvement and parental involvement. I chose these fields of work as a consultant due to my upbringing as a child of poverty. I realize that meaningful employment, in conjunction with a good education, can change a life forever. I would also like to thank Jackie "Yvonne" Norman of the Delaware County Public Assistance (Deceased) and Mike Bennefield of the State of Delaware Office of Employment and Training. Both of these individuals believed in my work and gave me early stage contracts to conduct our HYPE (Helping Youth Pursue Excellence) Program and BASIC (Building And Sustaining Internal Change) Job Readiness Training. Without their initial support, this book would not be possible. We did not disappoint them, our programs were some of the highest rated in our region and nationally. I would also like to thank one of my most caring customers, Workforce Solutions of the South Plains. I appreciate the on-going work relationship I have with Nate Bratcher, Carrie Meeks and the many employees of this wonderful organization. I enjoy "Thinking Outside of The Box" as it relates to engaging the long-term unemployed in meaningful job search strategies and motivation in their area. **Most importantly, the real-world care they have for their clients. It is unusual to see.**

Lastly, I would like to thank my wife and supporter Pamela and our 4 children, Darrell Jr., Sophia, Alexander and Abigail. They are the fuel that keeps me focused on the work I do. Without their support, I do not know if I could effectively pull off the thousands of miles of plane travel annually that comes with my work. They keep me motivated to run the race.

Table of Contents

Foreword 6

Pillar 1-Perception Modification 13

Pillar 2-Habits Of Successful People 35

Pillar 3-Transferable Skill-Sets 52

Pillar 4-Turning Passion Into Careers 64

About The Author 83

Forward

My mother is one of the most amazing people on the planet. I say this not to be biased, but because of the positive impact she had on my life. As a child growing up in Syracuse, NY, I experienced abject poverty firsthand. I remember many Christmas seasons where I was not sure if we would receive gifts at all. Many days, we would struggle just to get meals on our table. It was not all to bad however because back then, the community supported the community. When times were hard, the community kicked in and helped one another. My mother, however; decided that enough was enough. She was tired of the on-going trap of poverty as a result of minimal education that led to limited job opportunities. In my family, many people dropped out of school during their middle school years. My mother made the decision to go back to school. As a result, she became the first person in our family to receive a high school diploma. She did not stop there, after getting the diploma she attended a workforce development program in my hometown. Upon graduation from the workforce program, she landed a job with a company by the name of John Deere. We were very excited for this was the first time that I could recall my mother obtaining meaningful employment. Up to this point it, was all entry-level jobs and welfare. A few months after employment, John Deere had a massive layoff. My mother lost her Job. Disappointed, but not knocked out of the game, my mother continued to search for employment. She frequented our local Job Center for assistance. An opportunity to work for a company by the name of Allegheny airlines presented itself. My mother did not have all the necessary skills to do the job that they required. *Even though she was not fully qualified for the position, she acquired valuable core competencies working as a secretary at John Deere that were transferable to this new position.* She also understood that she would have to learn new skillsets in order to succeed on the job. During the interview, she was able to sell them on her determination to become a success in this position, even though she did not have all the necessary qualifications to do the job. *She was willing to reinvent herself in order to gain meaningful employment.* It worked! my mother landed the job and it was working for the company Allegheny Airlines, which later changed its name to USair, Inc. that released us from the grip of poverty. Our situation changed almost immediately. My mother reinvented herself and as a result, she reinvented our lives.

My wife took a part time job working for a company that offers financial assistance to college students. The job was an entry-level customer service position. She previously worked as a systems engineer at a Nuclear Generation Plant in Pennsylvania. The plant had a layoff, and my wife, only on the job for a few years, was unemployed. **The new job was not her goal but it was a way to keep active in between jobs.** *My wife is the kind of person that once she takes on a job, she does not give it half effort.* She worked that entry-level customer service position in the same manner as she did working at the Nuclear Facility. She was so good at it, so good, she caught the attention of the President of the company. He would visit her booth from time to time to observe her excellent work. After a few months on the job, he asked Pam what she thought of the position and how it can be approved. **The President of a major college finance company was asking an entry-level employee for advice!** She thought about it over a few days and came to the realization that they did not have the best quality management systems in place at the company. She approached the President and gave him her thoughts on ways to improve service via enhanced quality management systems. He was impressed, and asked her to write a proposal just to see what she was thinking. She took a few weeks to research the possibilities, find out more about TQM and what it took it would take to implement a system of this nature at her company of employment. She submitted the completed document to the President and he said that he would look it over and get back to her. Two weeks later, she had heard nothing from him. She finally thought that he was simply looking for general information and the research documents was a way to gather some insights. Three weeks after receiving the document, the President approached my wife and asked her to come into his office for he had a few questions. After an exhaustive meeting with a plethora of questions, the President said to my wife the following, "Pam, I met with the board to share your research. Sorry for taking so long to get back to you but I wanted to wait until our monthly board meeting to discuss this with the company leaders. We have decided that we would like to offer you the position of Director of TQM to implement the strategies you outlined in the proposal." *My wife went from an entry-level part time customer service representative, to a high 5 figured Director of a start up department.*

What do my mother and wife have in common? *They reinvented themselves.* They looked at their core workplace competencies and used them to create new employment opportunities. They also were able to sell their competencies to prospective employers in such a way that they realized the benefit to hiring these two amazing women for their open positions.

In the case of my wife, it was creating something by using critical thinking skills to open up a door of opportunity. For my mother, it was her ability to sell her potential to the hiring manager in such a way that he felt comfortable that she could do the job. My wife's new position was beneficial to our family but my mothers--took us out of poverty. *Workplace success is the primary way to change life outcomes and eliminate poverty.*

This book is being written in a time where cities and states are looking for ways to help long-tem unemployed and dislocated workers find meaningful employment. *Billions of dollars are being spent every year by the governments in the USA and worldwide to address this on-going challenge.* **As a former highly successful workforce development provider, I say with all confidence that they are often barking up the wrong tree.** Another computer class or some other type of trade class is not going to fix the problem. *I believe that intensive soft skills development coupled with job and career reinvention are really the tickets to success.* I know this based upon my mother and wife's situation as well as running my BASIC Training (Building And Sustaining Internal Change) Job Readiness Program and our HYPE (Helping Youth Pursue Excellence) Youth Workforce Program. Our BASIC Training clients had some of the highest job retention rates of all WIA and JTPA programs in our region (and nationally.) *We were every successful and teaching our clients critical soft-skills as well as helping them analyze core competencies based upon previous work or volunteer experiences.* Many of our clients were first generation employed or long term welfare recipients. Often, we worked with dislocated workers and helped them to overcome barriers to employment after losing jobs. If a person has been on a job for many years, it can be a major challenge trying to reinvent. It becomes a process.

This book is also being written as a tool to help workforce development organizations and agencies as well as the clients themselves, develop innovative systems for job search success via reinvention soft-skills development, and enhancement of prospective employee core competencies. Working in the field hands in a hands on manner, helping thousands of long-term unemployed and youth workers succeed, I have a lot of experience helping clients identify and sustain meaningful employment. In the case of the youth, realize the importance of staying in school, decreasing risky behavior and embracing the importance of work to long-term life success and goals. It is my hope that this book will be a tool to help the organizations and people who have the greatest challenge in workplace success. The long-term unemployed and dislocated worker.

Format

The chapters in the books are not given the name "Chapter" but are to be viewed as "Pillars." The goal of each pillar is to act as an independent foundation to the reinvention process. ***In essence, each chapter can be immediately flipped to address a specific workforce reinvention need.*** In doing so, the process itself will be fluid. I sincerely hope this book helps clients and organizations worldwide achieve workforce development success. *It is in no way the gold standard, just insights from 20 successful years helping adults and youth gain meaningful employment.*

Pillar 1-Perception Modification

You often attract what you think about. What you embrace as truth, will often come true-Coach D

Henry Ford was an amazing human being. Many of us know him for the invention of the Model T automobile, but what most people do not realize is that he also invented the assembly line. This was his greatest invention. Most people also may not know as well that Ford only had a high school education. **What he lacked in education, he made up in critical thinking.** The funny thing about his story is this, he hired many highly educated men to run his company! A local newspaper once interviewed him and the interviewer asked Ford to provide one piece of advice that he would give to aspiring business owners or anyone else who desired success. Without blinking an eye, he looked at the interviewer and proclaimed, "If you think you can, or if you think you can't, you're right. **Henry Ford understood something that job seekers and workforce organizations worldwide need to understand as well, your thoughts are the primary pathway to job and life success.**

One of the greatest challenges we faced in our workforce development initiatives were words used by our clients. Words such as "I can't" or "I don't have enough experience" or "I have failed before" or many other self-degrading words. These words, once trapped in the mind, become self-fulfilling prophecies. They take ownership of your mind and in in some cases, your will. **We realized that our clients had serious perception problems as a result of past experiences, the words of others, the expectations of the community, or their lack of education, etc.** Why is it that Henry Ford, Steve Jobs and many great industrialist had the same level of education as some job seekers, but were able to build companies that hire millions of people? *My personal belief is one word-**Perception**. They believed they can and as result, their minds went to work making sure what they believed manifests itself in some way.* **They were driven to achieve the dream because they embraced the mindset that it can happen**. Granted, these are extreme examples for not many people in history accomplished what Ford or Jobs accomplished, but the purpose of this analogy is to focus on the mindset. Ervin "Magic" Johnson once said at an event I attended, "I am not the smartest person in the room, but none of you have more passion than me. I believe, and then I go after it." He is now one of the most successful African-American businessmen in the USA.

One of the first steps in the reinvention process is for people to modify perception of themselves and their job search potential. **Companies and organizations look to hire people who have self-confidence and self-determination**. They can tell in the interview if you lack these traits. Questions are asked to identify the most self-motivated people they can hire get the job done. Be it a cashier or an assistant manager, they are analyzing the way you think, to see if you are the best candidate. Our goal in this Pillar is to help you focus a key foundational building block in the reinvention process, **Perception Modification**. *If you can modify your perceptions of self and workplace potential, you can modify your outcomes.*

What Is Perception Modification

Perception Modification is the process of changing, or modifying the way you perceive a possibility or situation, in spite of potential barriers. **Put another way, I may have barriers to employment, barriers to life success, but I am going to change the way I see them.** I am going to focus on the positive possibilities until the possibilities become my reality. *I am not going to allow negative thoughts to dominate, I am going to will myself to see things out of the lens of possibilities.* This is a tool used by every great person that has ever existed. They refused to allow negativity to dominate their possibilities. This is a critical mindset for the job seeker to possess, especially during times where job market possibilities are limited.

Key Factors That Impact Long-Term Unemployed Perceptions

There are many factors that impacts the way a person dealing with long-term unemployment thinks. In order to modify these perceptions, we must first know what they are. Listed below are a few key factors.

Factor 1-Life Experiences-The way people see things is often connected to their life experiences. It is a great challenge to see potential in self, if a person did not grow up in a world that values potential. I had a lot of supportive people around me as a child, but I also had many negative influences. I found that as a young adult, the impact of these influences weighed on me. It took some years to break the bondage of these interactions, but take it from a person who ha experienced it firsthand, it is not easy. On the flip side of this, many of us may have had good life experiences personally, but we over assisted. Yes, over assisted. *Some parents have done so much for their children that as adults, they struggle to take personal responsibility.* If they fall short, it is always someone or something that is the reason. Life experiences, be they good or bad, can impact our perceptions.

Factor 2-Words-Words are some of the most powerful influencers on the planet. Words have shaped the history of mankind as we know it. Words such as "Give me Liberty of Give Me Death" or "Ask Not What Your Country Can Do For You, Ask What You Can Do For Your Country" are mainstays in all of our minds. The effective use of words can change the outcomes of a city, state or nation, as well as a person seeking a job. Oftentimes the long-term unemployed have been bombarded with negative words for so long, that they begin to see themselves out of the lens of others who think negatively about their potential. Words can hurt a person (no matter what the popular rhyme tells us) and can shape the way a person thinks.

Factor 3-Societal Expectations-Society as a whole is not very kind to people. It has the tendency to shine a negative light on individuals who have struggles in life. One of the major challenges we face is the onslaught of television shows that highlight quick success and riches acquired via reality shows, etc. Often people do not feel successful unless they achieve some type of high-level monetary gain per the images given to us on TV. This can be frustrating to people who are struggling to make ends meet. The images displayed on TV, in Music and beyond. I encourage my coaching clients and workforce customers to do what is necessary to minimize exposure to these things. They do not project an image of reality. Reality is simply this, the average person does not live like this. The average person has to find a job, get an education and pursue a career. To be quite honest, there is nothing wrong with being a person in pursuit of a job or vocation. *Good work provides a decent living and Hollywood frowns on this thinking.* **The sad part about this is we unfortunately see the end result of many people who buy into the Hollywood mindset. It is not always positive.** Getting a job is a good thing and can provide a meaningful life for you and your family. Don't buy into the crazy expectations of society. **You are a success if you gain meaningful employment.**

Many external and internal forces impact the way long-term unemployed shape perceptions. For many, there are multiple personal effects of long-term unemployment as well. Some of the effects people feel as a result of long-term unemployment are as follows:

Effect 1-Loss of Identity-"Personal identity and professional identity are intertwined to the extent that the person has defined themselves by what they do," says Denise Glassmoyer, PsyD, a doctor of clinical psychology and a family therapist in private practice in Scottsdale, Ariz. "For these people, the impact of unemployment extends well beyond the financial impact. **In addition to losing their job, there may be the overwhelming sense that they have lost themselves.** Many experience profound self-doubt accompanied by feelings of sadness, anger, anxiety and hopelessness."(1)

Identity and employment are not mutually exclusive. Especially for the long-term unemployed client and the dislocated worker. *If a person has been on a job for a long period of time, their identity is often connected to their job.* It can take a long time for them to overcome the challenges of losing their jobs.

Effect 2- Trauma-*A Gallup study in the Economic Journal found that those who were out of work for at least a year took longer to recover emotionally than those who had lost a spouse.* **The results showed quantifiable declines in their health, their self-esteem and their overall emotional well being.** Hardest hit: the middle class. Workers with lower level skills found other lower-skilled jobs. Want to feel worse? The impact of long-term unemployment extends well beyond the direct worker. A more recent study found that a child whose parent loses his or her job is 15% more likely to repeat a grade in school, according to the University of California Davis research team of economists Ann Huff Stevens and Jessamyn Schaller. (2)

Trauma from losing employment is highly challenging. It brings pain to many families. Trauma can often cause the long-term unemployed to struggle with the way they feel about themselves personally. Many, as a result of trauma, lose motivation for the job search.

Effect 3-Apathy-This is not your normal apathy from being lazy. *Often, this is the type of apathy that comes from fatigue over job search failure.* Failure so many times that giving up becomes a viable option. Apathy is crippling and limits potential. To the long-term unemployed, it can become a real challenge to job search success.

Modification

As we can see, there are many factors that shape the perceptions of the long term unemployed. *My belief however is simply this, the more one stays focused on the challenges, the more difficult it is to come up with solutions. This is why modification is so important.* **The problems may not go away immediately, but if I can re-frame the situation and see it out of a positive possibilities lens, eventually I should be able to mentally position myself to overcome the way I think, and focus on a different outcome.** This is no different that anyone else who is pursuing a goal. *Athletes often say that the biggest stumbling blocks they face are their own thoughts.* They realize that they often become more of a threat to themselves than the competition. *They also tell us that their best performance comes when they program their minds to see things differently. When they see winning as the primary goal and will themselves to victory.* I remember years ago speaking to a girls field hockey team at the University of Delaware. **This team was not supposed to be a contender at all in their division.** I provided them with a motivational speech, but most importantly, I had them conduct a visualization exercise. I had them close their eyes and we literally went through a scenario where they saw themselves winning each and every game. We visualized beating each team, one at a time. We walked through this process until we ended up at the conference championship and ultimately, they won that. **I had the girls open their eyes and run around the auditorium high fiving each other as though they really**

won the championship! It was mass pandemonium. These amazing young ladies unfortunately did not win the conference championship as we visualized because they lost their one and only game in the conference finals.! *Please keep in mind, they were not supposed to win many games at all!* **This example leads us to highlighting a few strategic perception modification steps to overcoming perception barriers to long-term unemployment:**

Strategy 1-Vlsualization (Writing A Vision)

Write down a vision for your future. Do not limit what you write down. The kind of life you want. The place where you want to live. The career that you really want. Write it in such a way that you can see it really happening. Look at what you wrote down on a daily basis. Analyze in such a way that you begin to believe it is possible. Below is an example that you can use for a blueprint:

5 Things I Visualize
1. Having a job or career that is financially rewarding and fulfilling
2. Moving into a nice home or apartment
3. Changing my families destiny
4. Taking nice family vacations
5. Saving for my future.

What Will It Take To Succeed?
1. Taking advantage of support systems from my local job center/workforce agency.
2. Getting workplace counseling if needed.
3. Finding friends who will support my dreams
4. Eliminating negative thoughts that try to penetrate my thinking.
5. Doing something towards my goals everyday. Realizing that meaningful employment is one of the top priorities, giving this quality time.

Exercise:

Take the time and go through this process for yourself. Again, do not place any limits on yourself.

5 Things I Visualize
1.
2.
3.
4.

What Will It Take To Succeed?
1.
2.
3.
4.

Visualization is powerful. All my professional life I've visualized. Prior to becoming an employment motivator, trainer and coach, I wanted to work in corporate sales. I saw sales representatives driving around in their company cars and this impressed me. I loved seeing them in their chic suits and talking on their cell phones, and from that, I realized there were certain levels of sales. Of course, I wanted to be in one of the key sales fields. After thorough research, I decided that I wanted to work in the medical sales field. I even knew what company I wanted to work for — Abbott Laboratories. Thus, I began to visualize myself being a top-rated salesperson for Abbott, building my customer base. At the time of this visualization, the medical sales field was primarily interested in hiring people who held degrees in life sciences. Realistically, since I had a degree in business, I shouldn't have been in contention to work for any medical firm, let alone a major one like Abbott.

The recruiter who was working for me told me that I'd need to acquire a few years of experience before I could even *consider* getting into the field. He said there was no way that a company in the medical field would hire me, because I didn't have the right credentials. I told him to continue to pursue such opportunities anyway, and I would deliver when the time came. He agreed, and continued to look for employment opportunities for me. Again, self-determination is a major selling tool.

One day, I received a phone call from him stating that he had an unbelievable opportunity for me, although he was sure I wasn't ready for it. Nevertheless, he thought an interview was warranted, even if it turned out to simply be practice.

"Don't expect in any way to get the job; just use it as a time to get an understanding of the process", I was told. I started to probe him for information about the opportunity. Finally, I persuaded him to tell me the location of the company. The moment he told me the location, I knew it was Abbott. After confirming it, I proceeded to tell him about my vision for working with this company. This was not just a coincidence, but a destiny. I had a vision to work there, and no one or no thing was going to deny me this position. *I had studied the company, their competition, products and services, divisions, and sales representative expectations. I was ready and determined, and preparation finally met opportunity.*

"I respect your enthusiasm, however, this is no ordinary company," the recruiter said. "You won't get this job, but let's give it a try."

I arrived at my interview prepared and determined. The district manager who interviewed me was stern and straightforward: she was a former army captain and demonstrated this kind of manner in the interview. She was respectful, but direct and firm, and asked me extremely difficult questions. However, I was prepared to answer them. I had this vision locked into my mind and was determined to show her that I was the man for the job.

At the end of the interview, she asked me if I had any questions for *her*. I replied, "Yes, I do." My next move was a major surprise, even to me. I realized this was it and I had to give it my all. "How's the interview process coming along?" I asked. "It's been tough; I've over one hundred resumes on my desk, and many more forthcoming." She responded. "I guess this must be somewhat of a demanding process for you?" I stated. "Yes, it is," she sighed. *"Well, I have an answer that can finalize the process for you. I notice that you have a lot of resumes on your desk. I also notice that you have a trashcan next to your desk. I recommend that you take the resumes and dispose of them in the trash can, because you don't have to look any further: your man is sitting right here.* "She looked at me in amazement. For about thirty seconds she simply stared at me, then got up, went to speak to the regional manager. I believe, said to him, "Our man's sitting in the room next door!"

Within a week, I was an employee of the company — the process normally takes a lot longer. I believe, to this day, that the only reason this happened the way it did, was because of the passionate vision that I had for the position. I refused to be denied, and this allowed all things to come together for good. That job turned my life around, an experience I'll never forget. *Having a vision can make the impossible seem possible, and all it takes is having a clear focus on what it is you want, thinking about it, and putting those thoughts into action.*

Strategy 2-Strategic Goal Setting

Many people have goals, but few are strategic. Having a goal to lose weight is not a goal. Having a goal to lose weight with strategic steps such as how many daily calories and I going to take in? What is my weight now and what will it be in a few weeks,? A few months? What will be some of the primary foods I will eliminate from my diet? *This is a real strategy, not simply putting down I want to lose weight.* Who doesn't?

Take the aforementioned visualization information you completed and add the following to it:
- Start Date
- Who Can Help?
- Action Steps
- Personal Benefits
- How I Will Reward Myself For Success?

This model takes what you visualize from concept to reality. Most people search for work do not have strategic goals and effective goal planning starts with shifting of mindsets. This is one of the critical pieces of the reinvention process.

Strategy 3-Commitment To Soft Skills Training And Synergy

Many job centers offer career and soft skills training and from my perspective, they go hand to hand. If I get all of the career training but I do not show up for work, interact as a team player, exhibit a good work ethic, etc., then getting and keeping employment is going to be a major problem. One of the major problems faced by employment organizations is keeping people in training programs.

Hard Skills Can Be Taught. Soft Skills Are A Matter of Choice

Your ability to show up on time, work in teams, go above and beyond, and do your job well is often a personal decision. Employers today see these skills as highly important in considering potential employees. In particular people that are reinventing themselves. In my programs over the years, the listed soft skills were the ones we spent the most time focusing on. They helped hundreds of our program participants find and keep meaningful employment.

1. Strong Work Ethic

Are you motivated and dedicated to getting the job done, no matter what? Will you be conscientious and give it your best?

2. Positive Attitude (Number 1-Coach D)

Are you optimistic and upbeat? Will you generate good energy and good will?

3. Good Communication Skills

Are you both verbally articulate and a good listener? Can you make your case and express your needs in a way that builds bridges with colleagues, customers and vendors?

4. Time Management Abilities

Do you know how to prioritize tasks and work on a number of different projects at once? Will you use your time on the job wisely?

5. Problem-Solving Skills
Are you resourceful and able to creatively solve problems that will inevitably arise? Will you take ownership of problems or leave them for someone else?

6. Acting as a Team Player
Will you work well in groups and teams? Will you be cooperative and take a leadership role when appropriate?

7. Self-Confidence
Do you truly believe you can do the job? Will you project a sense of calm and inspire confidence in others? Will you

have the courage to ask questions that need to be asked and to freely contribute your ideas?

8. Ability to Accept and Learn From Criticism
Will you be able to handle criticism? Are you coachable and open to learning and growing as a person and as a professional?

9. Flexibility/Adaptability
Are you able to adapt to new situations and challenges? Will you embrace change and be open to new ideas?

10. Working Well Under Pressure
Can you handle the stress that accompanies deadlines and crises? Will you be able to do your best work and come through in a pinch?

Strategy 4-Change Your Environment

One of my favorite movies is a movie by the name of "Akeela and the bee." It was about a young lady who was gifted in spelling be but challenged because she did not think she had the ability to win the Scripts Spelling Bee. Once she connected with several kids in another school who were talented and driven as she was, Akeela was able modify her perception and as a result, she won the Scripts Spelling Bee. **If you are in an environment that does not support your ability to excel, think about connecting with people, organizations and associations that will.** In most cities there are ample opportunities to connect with progressive minded people via Churches, volunteerism, non-profit organizations and the like. You can control your destiny by changing who you choose to associate with. Your future is truly in your hands.

Perception Modification Quotes

Here are several quotes I find are directly connected to the message of perception modification that I am trying to communicate.

> *As a single footstep will not make a path on the earth, so a single thought will not make a pathway in the mind. To make a deep physical path, we walk again and again. To make a deep mental path, we must think over and over the kind of thoughts we wish to dominate our lives.*
>
> **Henry David Thoreau**

> *The greatest discovery of my generation is that a person can change his life by changing his attitudes of mind.*
>
> **William James**

Great minds suffer violent opposition from mediocre spirits!

Albert Einstein

If you think you can or if you think you can't, you're right!

Henry Ford

First comes thought; then organization of that thought, into ideas and plans; then transformation of those plans into reality. The beginning, as you will observe, is in your imagination.

Napoleon Hill

Quotes are a powerful way to see how great thinkers think. I would encourage you to memorize several quotes that can assist you in your perception modification journey. I memorize many quotes personally to assure that I can remain self-motivated to do the work I do. As I need the quote in my own life personally or as a coach or speaker, I can pull it up. I will share powerful quotes all throughout this book just as a way of starting the process.

Reinvention Application

As an old commercial states: "The mind is a terrible thing to waste." Most people have no idea of the power of change they can create via perception modification. It has been hypothesized that the mind had 1000% the capacity of a computer! Please keep in mind that it was somebodies mind who thought of the computer! As you are looking to reinvent yourself, please keep these things in mind in your job search process:

1. Never doubt yourself
2. Do not let people belittle you or minimize your potential.
3. Practice positive thinking. Stay away from pessimism
4. Participate in Job Search and Soft Skills training classes. Show up everyday.
5. Stop making excuses. Excuses will take away precious time that you cannot get back.
6. Ask for help. Find people who will support you in your reinvention process.
7. Smile . Too many people look mad at life and this look will not take you far.
8. Find new circles to associate with. You cannot get a new result with an old mindset.
9. See the bigger picture for you and your family.
10. **Modify Your Perceptions!**

Pillar 2-Habits Of Successful People

Excellence is not a singular act, but a habit. You are what you repeatedly do!

Shaquille O'Neal

What is it that makes great people great? What is it that causes phenomenal internal and external success to come into a person's life? Why do some people seem to do things with little to no effort, and others seem to struggle? *The answer lies within the internal make-up of the person. The internal make-up of a person consists of the environmental and interpersonal stimulus that they experienced over a lifetime, and the habits that were formed because of this environmental stimulus.* This is my theory; however, I perceive it to be true.

In this chapter we will review a few insights that were touched on briefly in the first pillar. Reinvention is so affected by what we think and say that it is worth continuing down this journey. I hope you make the connection with what we are trying to communicate.

I had a cousin who unfortunately lost his life in a dreadful event. Several years prior to his death, he asked me something that still sticks in my mind, "I want to change, but I just don't know how to." I was young at the time and didn't have a great answer for him. Due to the environmental stimulus in his life, he formed bad habits that unfortunately resulted in his demise. I loved my cousin and hated to see him leave this earth, and I sometimes wish he were around now, so that I could give him better advice.

Habits can make or break a person. Millionaires are rich because of habits, drug addicts are addicted because of habits, students receive good grades because of habits, and parents are good or bad parents because of habits. A habit is defined by Roget's Thesaurus as an "activity done without thinking," or "a habitual way of living."

How Are Habits Formed?

Performing a certain activity over a prolonged period of time—repetition—primarily forms habits. The psyche becomes adjusted to this particular behavior, and in many ways, it becomes the norm. Kids born into impoverished situations typically take on the habits of their environments and reproduce them in their own lives. The corollary is that children born in loving households take on the characteristics of those households, and duplicate them in their own lives. Business people who've developed good business practices will often end up with successful businesses. On the other hand, business owners who develop bad habits typically go bankrupt within a relatively short period.

In order to form a good habit, you must practice doing good things. *This is really important to the job search process.* When I was younger, I developed the habit of saying what I *couldn't* do. My mother corrected this negative affirmation by making me say what I *could* do. I'm so glad that she did, because it made a vast difference in my life. She assisted in my development of positive habits that shaped the course of my life.

In this chapter, we're going to look at the habits of successful people, and how you can use these habits to help you in your reinvention process.

The three habits we'll analyze are:

1. Habitually Using Positive Words
The habit of speaking positively about your potential.

2. The Habit of Being Actively Involved
The habit of becoming involved with activities that propel your passion.

3. The Habit of Saying No To Time Wasters
The habit of saying "no" to activities that will take you off course.

Habit 1: Habitually Using Positive Words

In our youth-training program, HYPE (Helping Youth Pursue Excellence), we have a training module called "The Seed of Your Words." This module was developed to show kids the power of words. We start out by saying some common words like "pizza," and the kids respond, "good," "tasty," "delicious," or "would like some now." Then we say a word such as, "homework." The kids automatically give us a different response such as, "hard," "boring," "cuts into my video game time," or "a pain." Following that, we ask the question, "Why is it that when you heard the word 'pizza,' you gave us a positive response, and then when we said, 'homework,' you gave us a negative one?" We explain that both words impacted their internal thought system, in some way, to produce a response.

The words, themselves, were a form of stimulus. I believe that all words have this ability ... they have what I call "impact-ability." They have the ability to impact you positively or negatively. Words can be felt. Just as the training module states, "Words are seeds," the seeds go into the soil of your heart, and with the help of more words, continue to grow. Bottom line: words you say can make or break you.

As mentioned earlier, people who are looking to reinvent themselves talk about workplace possibilities and other things in an uplifting manner. They operate in the positive realm.

Words

As stated earlier, when I was a child, I had the habit of regularly saying, "I can't." It didn't matter what it was, I automatically said it. My mother would tell me, "Son, don't say you can't; say you can." For years we went back and forth. I would say, "I can't," and she'd respond, "You *can.*" Eventually, her continued persistence paid off, and I began to automatically say, "I can." It didn't matter how I felt inside, outside, or any side — I believed what my mother told me ...I can. This attitude has been a great foundation for success in my life, an attitude that's helped me as an athlete, student, father, and a husband. I never let obstacles stop me in any way, because I believe in my potential.

Words have a way of motivating you to action, and this is where the word "motivation" comes from. A motive is an inner state that energizes, activates, and directs behavior toward goals. Words are the fuel for our motives; what we say is what we become. This is why I love being a motivator. My words can cause a person to go for their goals in life. This is the same reason why you should say positive things regarding your career potential.

What you say about yourself is a direct indicator of what's inside of you. *In order for your reinvention process to take full form, it needs your cooperation.* Think about yourself for a moment and then answer the following questions:

- How do I feel about myself and why?
- What words do I use to describe myself and why?
- What are my values, and where did they come from?

- What are my standards, and where did they come from?
- What do I watch on TV, listen to on the radio? What am I allowing to penetrate my mind?

The answers to these questions will provide insight into the influence of words in your life. People who are looking to reinvent decide the words that go into their lives, versus allowing those words to simply slip into their subconscious mind. **From this point forward, think about what consumes your thinking, and realize that these words are shaping your perception of life and job potential.** Take control of words, and you can literally write your future.

Words And Our Environment

In some of our training classes, we conduct an unusual exercise: we ask people to lift their hands slowly and then lift them quickly; we ask them to sit up and then sit down; we ask them to smile and then frown. When we complete all of the activities, we ask them the question, "Why do you think we did this exercise?"

We obtain a variety of responses, but never do we receive the one we're looking for, so we proceed to tell them that the reason for this exercise is to show them how much they're in control. We gave them a stimulus (a command) and they responded — **they made the decision to respond to the stimulus; nobody made them do it**. The concept we're really trying to teach is that since you're in control, you can, by the use of appropriate words coupled with corresponding actions, direct yourself along the path you want to go. The average person doesn't realize this until it is pointed out. The majority of lives are spent under the influences of the opinions and words of others — values, standards, opinions, activities, and habits have been hand-delivered by other people. Self-direction has not been considered.

If you're going to reinvent, you *must* take charge of your own life. It's important to understand that you cannot progress forward, if you continue down the same path and regularly associate with people who lack passion. If you want to be a succeed, you need to change your environment. This doesn't mean you have to throw out the baby with the bath water; however, you do need to re-focus. The wrong environment, associating with people, places, and things that send the wrong message can be devastating. Negative words that come from this environment can have a damaging effect on the job search process.

In my first year of returning to college (I quit my first year), I started to associate with people who wanted to do everything *but* acquire an education. Their only mission was to party, hang out, and enjoy their newfound freedoms. Based upon my previous college experience, I should have known better. Eventually when I began to hang around new group of friends, the words that the older group used to keep me in their core were degrading. The guilt trips and attempts to force me to show compassion for their ways — the crab technique — kept me in the barrel.

This new set of friends who were more serious about their future. Most importantly, our conversations were more uplifting and motivating than the previous relationships. Most of my newfound friends went on to graduate from college, whereas the bulk of the previous group dropped out of college. Besides the activities in which we participated, the greatest difference in the relationships was the communication we established: we encouraged each other, and this made a world of difference.

Along with your own words, the words of others can a have significant impact on your life. You can be heavily influenced by other people, like it or not. If this is the case, it becomes increasingly more important to control and take charge of your environment; otherwise, it will be extremely difficult to succeed in your job search and reinvention efforts. Remember, your associations will inevitably impact the words you say about yourself, so whatever you do, think about whom you are around on a regular basis and make changes, if necessary. Your associations will have an impact on the words you internalize and hence impact your job search effort.

Habit 2: The Habit of Being Actively Involved

Initially, I couldn't understand it. I had a good message, was well prepared, and still had no business. "It just doesn't make sense," I used to say. My wife and I began to look over what we were doing. We asked around, asked for advice, and eventually came to a common-sense answer. Most people who were landing business contracts knew other people who referred prospective clients to them — simple, but true. Having a good product, excellent service, and choice location doesn't guarantee a customer base. What many fail to realize is, to the extent that you serve the community, the community will serve you. Please understand this statement that you will rarely hear as it related to job search. **Many times people get jobs via who they know.** People who know this try to connect with people of influence. **Bottom line: you have to become involved.**

It doesn't matter what your reinvention goals are. The more involved you are, the more people you'll meet, and the better your chances of success. Prior to this revelation, I had no idea what a board was, or its purpose. I now sit on several boards and chair some. I enjoy what I do. Many people now know what my business offers and regularly refer my services. **If I hadn't become involved, this would never have happened.** Don't get me wrong; I'm not telling you to become involved solely for reciprocity. I'm saying that it's a good way to share your reinvention goals with a multitude of people, as well as serving in your community at the same time. Passionate people want to be heard. They realize that it takes people to make their passion a reality. Everything we do in life is, in some way, connected to other people. If you're a scientist, your science can be a blessing to the nation. If you're a singer, your voice can provide motivation as well as comfort to many. If your love is banking, your financial knowledge can help people to establish a secure financial future. If you desire to be a law-enforcement officer, you can protect people from harm and danger by providing a secure environment for all. No matter what your job pursuits are, they can positively impact upon the lives of others. This is why it's key for others to know about you and your work desires. Simply keeping it to yourself isn't going to do anything for anyone. You need to get out, be involved, and let the world know about your job search goals. Get involved now! Don't wait until all your ducks are in a row …there will never be a perfect time. The time is *now*.

Start attending local meetings relevant to your job search process. Keep one thing in mind: *becoming involved doesn't mean giving up all of your time,* it simply means keeping connected to individuals and activities that can help push your job search forward. Here's an example of how to become involved:

Reinvention Goal-To Become A Manager of A Restaurant
Timeline -Accomplish this within a 4-month period

Organizations And Activities In Which I could Become Involved:-I will check and see if there is a local restaurant association. If yes, I will see if it is possible to volunteer to help with some of their events. I will identify which type of restaurant in which I would like to work. I will check to see what type of community activities they support and try to show up when they are out in the community. I will try to get to meet people of influence within the business using this technique.

By doing this, you will meet owners of restaurants and possibly managers of chains. By using your skills to volunteer, you can gain access to influential people.

Being involved gives you energy, encourages you to go for the gold, and provides fuel for the fire. Just sitting around promotes frustration and a sense of hopelessness. **Your career desire will only take place if you add the dimension of *action*.** Passionate people are constantly on the move. They're involved and going for it on a daily basis.

Habit 3: The Habit Of Saying No To Time Wasters

My son's vocabulary was excellent for a two-year-old, but the one word he mastered more than others was the word "No." I'd ask him to do something, and with a determined look on his face, he'd look at me and say, "Nnnnooo," drawing it out for masterful effect. I'd ask him again and again, but I would hear, "Nnnnnoooo." Naturally, Daddy would have to correct this behavior at some point; however, my son was determined to stand his ground, and his opinion was unwavering: he was defending what he believed.

As a passionate person, you must know when to say, "No." Even though we recommend becoming involved, please keep in mind you cannot do everything—a sense of realism must be in place.

There was a time when I simply had too much activity in my life. I was trying to help everyone, assisting where and when I could, *and* maintaining my own personal life. I began to feel overwhelmed, and over the years, I became unproductive. I realized I had a major problem; I just couldn't say, "No," to people. Constantly, I was approached for assistance of one sort or another, and my invariable response was, "Yes." This left me with little time to pursue my dream in life.

Saying, "No," to people who are used to hearing, "Yes," all the time is a very difficult process. For people with an amicable personality, it is *extremely* difficult. When working on your job search process, a higher value is placed on time; thus, it becomes impossible to do *everything*. When pursuing employment, we must realize that time also becomes one of our best friends, so we must become comfortable saying, "No." Start doing this immediately. Practice it this week. *When you feel the urge to say, "Yes," say to the person in a diplomatic way, "I'm sorry, but due to my schedule, I must say no to this opportunity. I wish you the best in finding someone to assist you."*

Once you make this statement, stand on it, and don't deviate. My wife always says the following, "When you have a compelling *yes*, 'No,' becomes easier to say." Your compelling *yes* should be your passion for finding meaningful employment. Don't compromise this for anything.

Reinvention Application

Habits can be bad or good. In this pillar (or chapter) we wanted to focus on the habits that cause successful people to accomplish a life of achievement . If you've developed bad habits during your lifetime, with hard work and diligence, you can eliminate them. ***Your habits directly correlate with your job success future.*** If you're going to do anything on a consistent basis, make sure it's something that will propel you forward. Determined people decide their habits — they're in control of themselves, and therefore their future. Make it a priority to establish the listed habits in your life; you will be thankful that you did.

Psyche And Patterns

Habits are primarily formed by patterns you establish by doing or associating with the same thing over and over again. Your psyche becomes adjusted to this particular behavior, and it becomes the norm in your life. Here are a few habit defining areas of note:

- Passionate individuals view themselves and their life possibilities in an uplifting manner, instead of a derogatory one.

- Everything we do in life is connected to other people in some way.
- Even though we recommend becoming involved, please keep in mind you cannot do everything—a sense of realism must be in place.
- Having a vision can make the impossible seem possible. You must have clear focus on what it is you want, then think about it, and put action to your thoughts.

Habits of Successful People Quotes

I never could have done what I have done without the habits of punctuality, order, and diligence, without the determination to concentrate myself on one subject at a time.

Charles Dickens

The people you surround yourself with influence your behaviors, so choose friends who have healthy habits.

Dan Buettner

Successful people are simply those with successful habits.

Brian Tracy

Pillar #3-Utilizing Core Competencies And Transferable Skill-Sets

It may be hard for an egg to turn into a bird: it would be a jolly sight harder for it to learn to fly while remaining an egg. We are like eggs at present. And you cannot go on indefinitely being just an ordinary, decent egg. We must be hatched or go bad.
C. S. Lewis

As mentioned previously, one of the greatest challenges for dislocated workers is the mindset that is developed as a result of being on the same job for long periods of time. **Many get discouraged when they do not succeed and henceforth give up the job search process.** *In their minds, they think that this is the only type of employment that they can pursue.* For instance, if I worked in HR for 25 years, the only job I am qualified for is "HR." They often go out into the marketplace confident after a layoff that they can find a job in this employment sector. What they often fail to realize is that while working in HR, they may have picked up many skill-sets that have the ability to open to door to new job possibilities. Because they were not exposed to this information, they became discouraged and oftentimes, as we hear in the news, give up on the job search process.

The US Department of Labor pointed out that a record 89,3024,000 people gave up the job search process during the great recession. **Many gave up, I am sure; because they could not find a job in their fields.**

This chapter is one of the critical chapter sin our book for it is going to show job seekers how to analyze their core competencies. What skills do I possess as a result of things I learned in previous employment or volunteerism. What have I learned from past experiences that I can now use as a possible job search opportunity.

Using my wife Pam as an example, if you recall, she reinvented herself from a systems engineer into a Director of TQM. **She had no actual TQM experience, but excellence in her Entry Level position, as well as experiences she gained as an Engineer, helped open the door to this new possibility.** Listed below are key strategies for using transferable skill-sets to open job opportunity doors as well as reinvent yourself and your future. I have personally helped hundreds of job seekers via coaching and workshops using what you are about to read. It can become a formula for reinvention success.

Strategy #1-Transferable Skill-Set Analysis

Analysis of transferable skill-sets from previous employment or volunteer work is a valuable tool for increasing new employment opportunities. **For the sake of definition, transferable skill-sets are skills learned from the aforementioned categories.** A quick example of this is if I worked in HR for a major organizations, not only did I learn HR functions, I might have learned data management, which could open the door to a different job opportunity that utilizes this skill. Again, using Pam as an example, lets look at the many possibilities via analysis that could have benefitted her in landing employment in a totally different field. It is important to understand that the key here is not to limit yourself. Take the time and write down all the possible skill sets that can come from an experience. I will explain why this is important shortly.

Job: Systems Engineer
  Transferable Skill-Sets:
  1. *Management of other people*
  2. Management of systems
  3. Critical thinking skills
  4. High end communications
  5. Meetings management
  6. Time management

7. Troubleshooting
8. Project management
9. Organization
10. Leadership

For those of you who may think, "I have never been a systems engineer. That is a little out of my league. Lets look at a simple volunteerism opportunity and transferable skill-sets that can be derived from it.

Volunteer Opportunity-Helping To Plan A Family And Friends Day At Our Hospital

Transferable Skill Sets:
1. Communications
2. Marketing
3. Teamwork
4. Planning
5. Management
6. Analysis

We can look at many more of these but hopefully you see the direction we are going. Now it is your turn. Take a few moments and identify 5 transferable skills that you may have developed in a past job or volunteer opportunity. If you feel led to, you can do this with multiple career or volunteer opportunities in mind. Once completed, we will show you how to position this information for future job possibilities.

Job or Volunteer Work:_____

Transferable Skill-Sets:

1.
2.
3.
4.
5.

Strategy #2-Capabilties Resume

Once you have identified several transferable skill-sets possibilities, the next step is to place this in writing to identify possible work opportunities. Please keep in mind, when Pam provided her employer with a proposal for a new department, there was nothing that supported she had the experience in building this department. What was in the information were the insights she offered based what she learned in past work experiences. *Her transferable skill-sets (core competencies) and current work ethic were good enough for the employer to feel comfortable offering her the job.*

One way for you to tell your story is via a **capabilities resume**. A capabilities resume is different that a regular resume for it focuses on capabilities, or transferable skill-sets, more than past work titles, etc. Below is an example of what a capabilities resume could look like. Again, this is an example, yours could look totally different:

John Doe
1120 Job Street
Employment, TX 21001
info@findajob.com
806-222-2222_

Summary

A hard working and passionate professional with a unique combination of workplace experiences in management and customer experience. I am a diligent employee looking for a career opportunity within my capabilities.

Professional Goals

To pursue a job in customer service for a local business or organization. To help my future employer achieve their organizational goals By providing top quality customer service to their customers or clients.

Education

High School Diploma-Texas Tech High School 2005.

-Customer Service Training-Walmart 2007

-Relationship Building Workshop-John Jim Church 2011 ----Reinvention-The Pathway To Job Search Success Workshops-Dallas Job Corp-July 2014

Capabilities And Skills

Based upon work, volunteer and personal experiences, I posses the following

    -Teamwork

    -Management of People

    -Critical Thinking Skills

    -Organization

    -Leading Meetings

    -Training

    -Conflict Resolution

Work Experience

2007-2010 Walmart-Customer Service Representative

Made sure the customers have a great experience shopping at Walmart. Won customer service rep of the year in 2004.

2011-2014 Lubbock General Hospital Patient Services Representative-Helped patients commit to their medical care. Proposed various strategies to make sure they followed through on suggestions made by the doctors.

References
Provided upon request.

Social Media
LinkedIn Page: LinkedIn Linked.com/in/johndoe
Facebook: facebook.com/johndoe.

Notice how prior to mentioning workplace experience, you are highlighting your capabilities or transferable skill sets. *This is a very important shift from normal resume writing.* **The primary reason why is you are trying to highlight your capabilities for the interview, not your past employment.** Of course, in an interview you will be asked about past work, but if you can clearly articulate your strengths based upon transferable skill-sets, or capabilities first, the hiring manager may be willing to overlook lack of experience. They very well may look at your potential first.

Strategy 3-Writing Your Capabilities Resume And Interview Practice.

Based upon what you wrote regarding your transferable skill-sets, take a few moments and write a capabilities resume. Fill in the following information to practice doing this:

Name:

Address:

City: **State:**   **Zip:**

E-Mail:

Phone:

Summary:

Capabilities And Skill-Sets

Based upon work, volunteer and personal experiences, I posses the following skill-sets:
1.
2.
3.
4.
5.

Work Experience:

    1.

    2.

    3.

References

Interview Practice

Once you complete your capabilities resume, ask a friend or family member to allow you to practice the interview process, in particular the part where you describe your transferable skills-sets. For instance, you might take your completed capabilities resume and ask the mock interviewer to ask you the following questions:

1. Tell me about your work experiences, what strengths do you possess?
2. What specific skills do you offer that would make you good for this job?
3. I notice that you do not have a lot of experience for this type of work, why should we consider hiring you for this work?
4. What makes you the best candidate for this job?

All of your responses to these questions should be directed back to your capabilities or transferable skill-sets. Remember, you are not trying to sell them on your work experience, you are trying to sell them on your potential. Your transferable skill-sets are your potential. It tells the prospective employer that even though this person does not have the experience, they have the skill-sets to learn the position. In the process of reinventing yourself, this insight is golden.

Reinvention Application

This is one of the most important components of the reinvention process. *Please take this pillar very seriously if you plan on reinventing your career path.* Remember to:

- Focus on your skill-sets. Sell them with passion.
- Write a clear and concise capabilities resume. Don't focus on your work experience, focus on your capabilities.
- Practice. Act as tough you are a salesman selling yourself. Nobody should be able to sell you better than you!
- Be confident. Confidence and passion sells employers. If they see you have the drive and

determination to succeed, they will give you a chance.

You were born to win, so don't think you are going to lose. See losing as a non-option. Reinvent yourself and as a result, you will reinvent your future potential.

Core Competencies And Transferable Skill-Sets Quotes

I believe that one defines themselves by reinvention. To not be like your parents. To not be like your friends. To be yourself. To cut yourself out of stone.

Henry Rollins

When we are no longer able to change a situation, we are challenged to change ourselves.

Dr. Victor Frankl

Change is the law of life. And those who look only to the past or present are certain to miss the future.

John F. Kennedy

You must take personal responsibility. You cannot change the circumstances, the seasons, or the wind, but you can change yourself. That is something you have charge of.

Jim Rohn

Pillar #4-Reinvention-Turning Passions Into Careers

Purpose is the key to fulfillment
Dr. Myles Munroe

We hear a lot of talk of the subject of this thing called purpose. There are many books (My first book was entitled, *How To Find Your Passion And Make A Living At It*) written to address this subject. Without a doubt, the majority of people at some point begin to think about this subject. I am truly a living example of a person who found their passion and make a living at it. Nothing, and I do mean nothing excites me more than motivating people to maximize their career, education and life potential. When people I coach or train people to gain meaningful employment, find and live their passions, succeed in business, buy a home and contribute in a major way, I feel like jumping through the roof. Dr. Myles Munroe, someone I call, the "Father of Purpose", introduced the world to this one truth, "we were all born with a gift that can be turned into a career, which has the potential to create to a better world for all." Sports stars have found their passions. Celebrity have found theirs. Many people we see on TV, singing the songs we love and much more, have found a calling or vocation that gives them a sense of meaning in life. I shared with all of my BASIC (Building

And Sustaining Internal Change) and HYPE (Helping Youth Pursue Excellence) program participants that they were born with brilliance in mind. They have something inside of them that if tapped into, can ultimately become a career or vocation that can change the lives that they live. *I am going out on a limb writing this chapter for I know that the first and foremost goal you have as a job seeker is to find meaningful employment.* **Please keep doing this but in conjunction with this goal, we would like to for you to begin thinking about what gifts or talents you have that could possibility to be turned into a career.** In my trainings and coaching, I spend copious time trying to teach my clients the process of passion identification and application. Listed below are a few areas we analyze in my coaching and training sessions. Hopefully they can be helpful to you in your passion pursuits.

Passion Identification-Passion Pathways

Over the years I have found that there is no single way to find your passion. When I first started sharing this message, I primarily used one method that I thought would work with everyone. I was incorrect and sincerely apologize to anyone who was challenged by this methodology. After researching, asking questions of my audience and thinking about the process in general, I identified five ways people typically find their passion and purpose in life. It is my sincere hope that this model of discovery will help in your quest to live a purpose filled life. One of the pathways "Trauma" is not the preferred method of finding it; however, many people do find it this way--unfortunately. Harriet Tubman found her purpose as a result of the trauma of slavery. She made it her life's mission to end it. **Many people overcome drug addiction and spend the rest of their lives making sure other people do fall into this trap.** Since it is not one that is typically relevant to job search, I will not include it is this book. The remaining four pathways are:

1. Lifetime Infatuation
2. Influence of Others
3. Vision and Introspection
4. Frustration

Pathway # 1 — Lifetime Infatuation

The Wright Brothers best exemplified this method. When they were little boys their father gave them a toy helicopter upon his return from a long mission. The toy helicopter gradually became their favorite toy, and they soon concluded that it was more than a toy, it had become an infatuation. The helicopter was a concept at the time, but this concept caught their attention. They were mesmerized by it. Even though aeronautics did not exist during their time, they developed the passion to create an airplane. This passion stayed with them all of their lives. Since they couldn't shake this idea that was considered impossible during their era, they moved to Kitty Hawk, NC to pursue this passion that they could not shake. As we all know, they invented the airplane, and all of us have benefited in some way from their ingenuity, whether we have taken a journey by plane or purchased fruit flown in from Brazil. This is what I mean when I say lifetime infatuation. **It is something that you are infatuated with**. It is something that moves you to action and causes you to dream the bigger dream. Your infatuation does not have to be as extensive as the Wright Brothers. You may have had an infatuation with cosmetology but gave up on it. You may been infatuated with space travel, but someone talked you out of it. Or you may have had a dream of becoming a business owner and lost the confidence to move forward. The significant point is that you still think about it. You can't seem to shake it; this is a sign that it is an infatuation, which can lead to a life's purpose and passion.

Exercise

Answer the following questions to determine whether you have an infatuation. If you do not have an answer to the questions, then this method may not be for you.

1. Do you regularly dream of a career path that you are currently pursuing? If so, describe it.

_____
_____
_____
_____

2. Do you have an idea or invention that you can't seem to stop thinking about? Have you wondered why no one else has ever discussed or invented it? What is it?

_____
_____
_____
_____

3. Do you regularly tell your friends about a dream that you have even though you are not currently pursuing it? For example, have you dreamed about restoring a classic car so beautifully that you imagine people clamoring for your services to restore their cars as well? Describe the dream?

_____
_____
_____
_____
_____

Lifetime infatuation is a major factor in passion identification for many people. However, as indicated earlier, it is not the only method.

Pathway #2 — Influence of Others

Years ago I attended a function in Chester, PA. at which the keynote speaker was Dr. Myles Munroe. **From the moment he opened his mouth, I hung on to every word he spoke**. He passionately discussed passion and purpose in such a powerful way that I was captivated for two full hours. One of his speech statements still resonates today: *"Where purpose is not known, abuse is inevitable."* He then went on to explain that: *"Purpose is the key to fulfillment."*

Years later I attended another event and the speaker was the world-renowned motivational speaker Zig Ziglar. Just as Dr. Munroe had captivated me with his powerful speech, Mr. Ziglar enthralled me as well. Both men influenced me in a way so powerful that I decided that I wanted also to become a motivator of people — just like them.

Who are the people that move you? Do you get excited whenever you hear a famous artist, great speaker, businessperson, teacher or professor? Does your heart jump when you see animal documentaries on television? If so, this may mean that you are being influenced by an area which or individual who is in involved in your life's calling. Many people find their passion through the influence of others. By observing others working in their field of expertise, many people become mesmerized and can see themselves in that same field. Answer the following questions to determine whether this is a method that best fits you.

Exercise:

1. Does your heart jump every time you see an individual working in a certain area of expertise? What is it?

2. Are there certain shows (cooking, art, history etc.) on television that seem to capture and keep your attention? Describe them?

3. Are there certain individuals you know who have the same interests as you? Do you get excited about having conversations with this person on the topics related to the common interest?

Once again, this is a major area of passion discovery. Hopefully it will shed some light on your life passion or purpose.

Pathway # 3 — Vision Introspection

This is the most research intensive of all of the methods. When I first started to share the message of passion, it is the one I used exclusively. To use this method, you simply start to write a journal. You record in your journal your life's activities, dreams, goals, relationships and more. The purpose of this method is to see patterns and commonalities in your life. Typically, no matter what direction a person takes in life, his or her passion keeps pulling like a magnet. As a passion pursuer, you may experience this regularly. YOUR PASSION IS RECOGNIZED BY PEOPLE ALL AROUND YOU. It is "in your face" constantly; however, you simply pass it off as a hobby or good thought. Yet introspection brings it to life. By journaling your life, you start to see the pathway opening wide. Some of the questions to consider in the journaling process are as follows:

1. When your friends make the statement "you missed your calling," what is this "calling" they are referring to?

2. What activities that benefit others do you en- gage in naturally, effortlessly, without thinking?

3. What activities are you regularly involved in?

4. What do you love to do so much that you could start by doing it for free?

The vision/introspection process can be a more challenging way to find your passion, but it is a fun journey. If you feel as though this is method for you to use, buy a journal and start the process. Devote time to this process at least four or five times a week.

Passion Pathway # 4 — Frustration

Harriet Tubman, the slavery abolitionist best exemplifies this method. For years she was a slave in the southern plantations. But after years of toiling as a slave she grew weary living of such a meager and demeaning existence. Better yet, she became FRUSTRATED. In her frustration, she found her purpose in life: to become a Moses for slaves during the 1800's. In fulfilling her life's calling, she led more than 300 slaves to freedom by way of the Underground Railroad system. Because of her efforts and those of people such as Thomas Garret and William Still in her Circle of Passion then, many African-Americans are free to live their dreams in this country today. Thank God she became frustrated. What are you frustrated with? Are you tired of seeing people waste away by spending their years doing drugs and other life destroying activities? Do you dislike the way our government is currently running Social Security or Child Care services, and do you plan to become involved in politics or some type of advocacy organization to do something about it? Would you like to work to reestablish family values in this country? Are you disheartened by the way people are overwhelmed by their debt, and would you like to create a system to help people manage their money more efficiently? *Many times your frustration is your passion crying out loud.* It could be something that you and only you were born to do in your own particular manner. Even though other people might be doing it, they will never, ever do it like you. It is your unique gift. Answer the following questions to see whether this method of passion discovery works best for you:

1. Is there something in society you want to fix?

2. Can you see yourself spending the rest of your life doing this?

3. What will be the benefit to people or to the country if you are able fix this problem?

4. How will mankind be improved by having you work on this endeavor?

Frustration is an unusual yet powerful way to find your passion. Many people have used this route, and hopefully, this method can enlighten you. *So, from now on don't look at frustration as something that is only aggravating and negative. It could very well be your life's passion shouting out loud!*

Advancing The Call

Did you find that one of these pathways worked better for you than another? If your answer is yes, GREAT! Keep analyzing the process and attempt to bring clarity to your passion. If your answer is no, ask for help! Chances are you may need a counselor or advisor or coach at your local Job Center to further assist you in this process.

Passion Mapping™

Another exciting development I have included in the passion journey is the process of Passion Mapping, which increases the career options with which you can work within your passion. Once you have identified your passion via the Passion Pathways, there are many directions you can pursue. Passion Mapping is the process of mapping out multiple career or job possibilities based upon a passion you identified. It also highlights the need for additional education and possible role mentors you can pursue. Look at an example of a Passion Map as a way of example:

Passion: Education

Mapping Possibilities:
1. Teacher
2. Author
3. School Counselor
4. Tutor
5. School Hall Monitor

Relevant Education:
1. Possible Bachelors Degree in Education
2. Associates Degree in Social Work
3. Substitute Teacher Training

Possible Mentors
1. My brother-he is a teacher
2. The Principal at my kids school
3. My Pastor who is on the school board.

Passion Mapping Process

As you can see this is not a complex process. Our program participants went through an extensive training on this subject and many of their lives and careers were changed as a result. Take a few moments and use the same format using a passion you identified in the Passion Pathways Exercise to create your own map.

Passion:

   Mapping Possibilities:

     1.

     2.

     3.

     4.

Relevant Education (Academic Needed)

     1.

     2.

Possible Mentors (People Who Can Help)

     1.

     2.

     3.

This is a very simplistic process to a very complex and focused activity. Once your passion is identified and mapped out, the key to turning it into a career is to develop a strategic goal.

People who find meaningful employment via reinvention are often excellent goal-setters. *They are focused, refuse to waste time and on-point.* In order to reinvent yourself, you must be focused as well. **In order to achieve new results, you need to do new things. You cannot operate in a** business as usual mode and think that you are going to achieve significant career outcomes.

You Must:
- Be focused
- Plan
- Network with people who can help
- Create new friendships
- Monitor your goals and expected outcomes

Take a few moments and fill out the goal sheet listed below. It will help you in your quest to take your passion and make a career out of it. Without goals, it will be very difficult to achieve your job search goals. Go to the next page and fill out the goal-planning sheet.

Goal: To Turn My Passion Into A Career-Reinvent Myself

Timeline: Start Date: _____ Completion Date: _____

Action Steps (What I Need To Do)	**Date Completed**

1.

_____

2.

_____

3.

_____

4.

_____

5.

_____

Resources to Consider

Resource	How Can They/It Help

1.

2.

3.

Benefits of Goal Attainment

Self:
_____

Friends:
_____

Family:
_____

How Will I Reward Myself?

_____

_____

_____

_____

Once you go through this process you are well on your way to achieving your career passion. In doing so, you will be well on your way to success. **I know that this was a stretch pillar but one that I wanted to provide that was different and far-reaching.** This book, as aforementioned, was written in such a way that each and every pillar (chapter) operates independently. If you think you have the drive and determination to go for it, pursue your passion with focus and vigor. I personally did, and now you are reading my book. Hundreds of thousands of people have! I look at my life and it is amazing to me that today I am now an internationally acclaimed speaker, trainer, coach and author. I have been invited to share my expertise with audiences and organizations worldwide. I quickly tell people that it was because I found my passion. If not, you would not be reading this book for it would not have been written. If I can do it, so can you. What is your passion?

Reinvention Application

I wrote this book as a result of my belief that people can take control of their job search process. I have helped so many people succeed in life that my mindset is bent on the belief that anything is possible. In order to turn your passion into a career:

- Analyze the pathway and mapping process
- Develop a Dream Team of people who can support you (2-3 People)
- Set goals and timelines
- Stick to your goals
- Say to yourself daily, if someone else can do it, so can I.

If you can do these things and do them effectively, not only will you reinvent yourself, you will change the course of your future. Realize, It can be done, so go out and do it!

Passion Quotes

A great leader's courage to fulfill his vision comes from passion, not position.

John Maxwell

Don't ask yourself what the world needs. Ask yourself what makes you come alive and then go do that. Because what the world needs is people who have come alive.

Howard Thurman

With out passion you don't have energy, with out energy you have nothing.

Donald Trump

About The Author

Darrell "Coach D" Andrews is an internationally recognized motivational strategist, author and career-life coach. His books, *How To Find Your Passion And Make A Living At It* and *The Purpose Living Teen-A Teen's Guide To Living Your Dreams,* have transformed thousands of individuals and organizations worldwide. His story, *5 Garbage Bags and a Dream* is one of the top stories in the national best seller *Chicken Soup For The African-American Soul.* As a speaker, career-life coach and trainer, he has been invited to motivate, train and consult some of the nation's top education institutions, workforce development organizations and non-profit associations. He has shared the stage with some of the foremost thought leaders in the world. He is also the developer of the H.Y.P.E. (Helping Youth Pursue Excellence) and B.A.S.IC. Training Job Readiness Programs. *HYPE* was one of the top-rated contracted youth programs nationally under the WIA (Workforce Investment Act) Grant. Coach D's *B.A.S.I.C* (Building and Sustaining Internal Change) Training was a successful JTPA Job Readiness training program for Dislocated, TANF and unemployed job seekers. Coach D's highly strategic workshops have helped thousands of career and job seekers at workforce development organizations, schools districts and college campuses throughout the USA, Canada and the Caribbean connect their personal passions to careers and businesses. Coach D received his CSP (Certified Speaking Professional) designation from the National Speakers Association and the Global Federation of Speakers. Less than 600 speakers worldwide have received this special accreditation. For close to two decades he has been a regular expert speaker and trainer at conferences, school districts, workforce development agencies and education based events worldwide.

Coach D has been a regular guest on many radio and television programs. He has been featured on MSNBC, Fox News, The Black Enterprise Report, The Tavis Smiley Show, Comcast Cablevision's "Your Morning" Talk Show to name a few. His life's philosophy has been the same for close to two decades, "It is not what you have accomplished in your life that counts-but what others are able to accomplish because of your life.

Lastly and most importantly, he has been happily married to the love of his life Pamela for 20+ years and is the proud father of Darrell Jr, Sophia, Alexander and Abigail. His family is truly his pride and joy.

Booking Contact Information
Darrell Andrews Enterprises
Phone: (302) 834-1040
Fax (302) 832-6127
e-mail:info@coachdspeaks.com
www.coachdspeaks.com

Service	Description
Reinvention-The Pathway To Job Search Success Workshop For Clients	Participants will go through an introspective, yet interactive and informative workshop helping them to create a plan of personal reinvention that lead to enhanced job search success. Can be conducted anywhere from ½ to 2 days.
BASIC (Building And Sustaining Internal Change) Week Long or Quarterly Workshops.	Invited Coach to your site to conduct multiple soft-skills trainings for your long-term unemployed. Workshops are typically ½ day for a period of one week. Many organizations book Coach D for quarterly trainings thereafter.
Staff Development or Motivation	Book Coach D to train your staff on best practices to engage your long-term unemployed or to motivate

	them to enhance client and personal success.
The Passion Mapping Seminar-Connecting Dreams To Careers-Youth	Contract Coach D to conduct a ½-full day seminar teaching WIA and Summer Youth the process of identifying passions that can be connected to future career and life success. This is a highly motivational, hands on event with a plethora of best practices.
Career or Leadership/Goal Coaching	Invite Coach D to your location to conduct a group coaching session for workforce clients, staff or organizational leadership. Coach D's coaching sessions are design to encourage accountability towards workplace goal achievement.
Bulk Book Orders	Use the form below or call the office to discuss ordering bulk copies of the book for your long-term unemployed or dislocated workers.

Reinvention-The Pathway To Job Search Success Order Form

0-50-$11.95 Per Book
51-100-$11.00 Per Book
101-500-$10.00 Per Book
500+$ 9.50 Per Book

Number of Books: _____   x **Cost:** _____
Price: _____ **Add 7% for Shipping:** _____
Order Total: _____

Three easy ways to place an order: CALL Toll-Free866-4-COACH-D (866-426-2243) Scan and E-MAIL: info@CoachDSpeaks.com or FAX TO: (302) 832-6127 Make Checks payable to : Darrell Andrews Enterprises, 1148 Pulaski Highway, Suite 197, Bear, DE 19701

Payment Options

☐ Cash   ☐ Check (made payable to Darrell Andrews Enterprises)   ☐ Credit Card

Name _____ Card Zip Code:_____
Credit Card # _____
CVV_____ Expiration Date _____
Signature _____

Shipping Information (Legible Please)

Name: _____
Address _____
City/State/Zip _____
Email Address _____
Telephone (   ) _____

References

(1) The effect of long-term unemployment-Wyatt Myers (Everyday Health)
(2) The trauma of long-term unemployment: Losing your job is just the start-Ann Brenoff

www.ingramcontent.com/pod-product-compliance
Lightning Source LLC
Chambersburg PA
CBHW071734040426
42446CB00012B/2354